LIFE CYCLES
Dragonflies

by Robin Nelson

first step nonfiction

Lerner Publications Company · Minneapolis

Look at the **dragonfly**.

There are many kinds of
dragonflies.

A dragonfly is an **insect**,
like an ant or a bee.

How does a dragonfly grow?

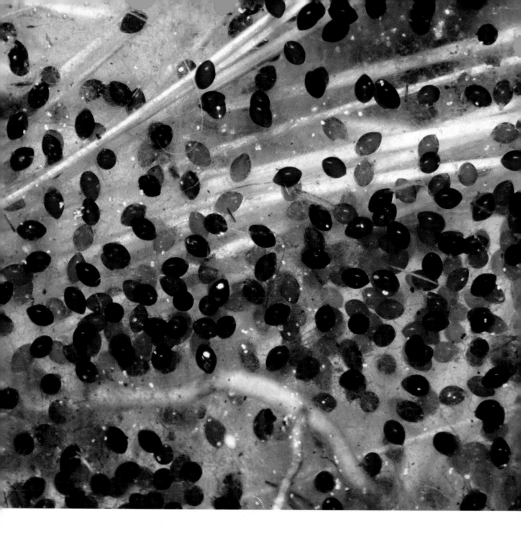

A dragonfly starts as an egg in the water.

A **nymph hatches** from the egg.

At first, the nymph looks like a bug.

It swims like a fish.

The nymph eats bugs and
fish and grows bigger.

It **sheds** its skin as it gets
bigger.

The nymph crawls out of the water.

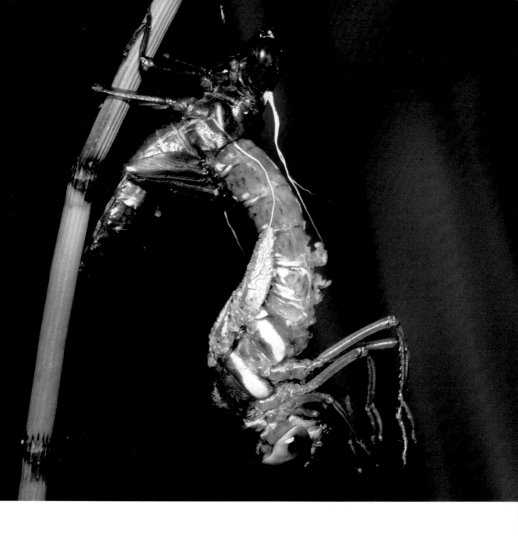

It sheds its skin one last time.

It becomes a dragonfly.

The new dragonfly dries its wings in the sun.

The dragonfly flies away.

It is fun to watch a
dragonfly grow.

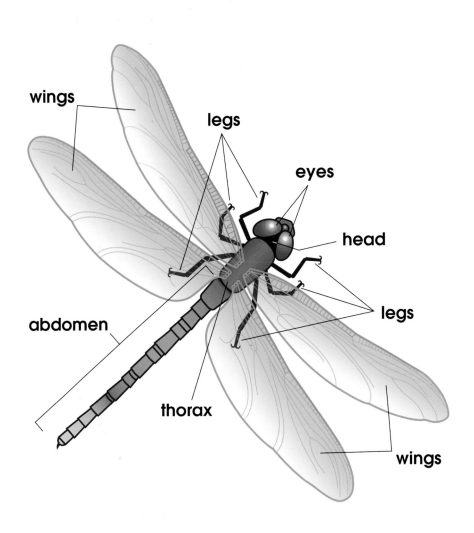

wings

legs

eyes

head

abdomen

legs

thorax

wings

Adult Dragonflies

Adult dragonflies have four wings to help them fly and six legs for walking and climbing. Their bodies have three parts, a head, a thorax, and an abdomen. They have two large eyes and strong jaws that they use to catch their food.

Adult dragonflies only live for a short time. They spend most of their life as nymphs. Once they become adults, female dragonflies lay their eggs, and a new dragonfly life cycle begins.

Dragonfly Facts

 Dragonflies are one of the largest insects.

 Dragonflies have been on Earth for over 300 million years. They were here before the dinosaurs!

 There are more than 2,500 different kinds of dragonflies.

 Dragonflies are excellent fliers! They can fly backward, in loops, or in one place.

 Dragonflies are helpful to humans because they hunt other insects that humans think are pests—mosquitoes, gnats, and flies.

 Dragonflies' large eyes help them to see really well. This is why it is so hard to catch a dragonfly. They can see you coming!

Glossary

 dragonfly – a large insect with a long body and four clear wings

 hatches – comes out of an egg

 insect – an animal with six legs and three main body parts

 nymph – a young dragonfly

 sheds – grows out of its skin

Index

The images in this book are used with the permission of: © Krzysztof Gorski/Dreamstime.com, front cover; © Adam Jones/Visuals Unlimited, p. 2; © Altrendo Nature/Getty Images, pp. 3 (top left), 22 (top); © Whit Richardson/Aurora/Getty Images, p. 3 (bottom right); © Tim Zurowski/ All Canada Photos/Getty Images, p. 3 (bottom left); © iStockphoto.com/Karel Broz, p. 3 (bottom right); © George Grall/National Geographic/Getty Images, pp. 4, 22 (center); © Tim Hall/ Stone/Getty Images, p. 5; © Rene Krekels/Foto Natura/Minden Pictures/Getty Images, p. 6; © Nature Production/Minden Pictures, pp. 7, 22 (second from top); © Dwight Kuhn, pp. 8, 9, 13, 14, 22 (fourth from top, bottom); © Gary Meszaros/Visuals Unlimited, pp. 10, 17; © Hans Pfletschinger/Peter Arnold, Inc., p. 11; © Neil Fletcher/Dorling Kindersley/Getty Images, p. 12; © Bob Elsdale/Photographer's Choice/Getty Images, p. 15; © Michael Durham/Minden Pictures/ Getty Images, p. 16.
Illustrations on pages 18, 20, and 21 are by Laura Westlund/Independent Picture Service.

Lerner Publications Company
A division of Lerner Publishing Group, Inc.
241 First Avenue North
Minneapolis, MN 55401 U.S.A.

Website address: www.lernerbooks.com

Library of Congress Cataloging-in-Publication Data

Nelson, Robin, 1971–
        Dragonflies / by Robin Nelson.
            p.   cm. — (First step nonfiction. Animal life cycles)
        Includes index.
        ISBN 978–0–7613–4066–9 (lib. bdg. : alk. paper)
        ISBN 978–0–7613–5167–2 (eBook)
        1. Dragonflies—Juvenile literature. I. Title.
    QL520.N45 2009
    595.7'33—dc22   2008025711

Manufactured in the United States of America
2 – BP – 6/1/13